KT-872-565

Role-play practice Spanish

Tony Whelpton

Chief Examiner, GCSE French, Southern Examining Group

Daphne Jenkins

Reviser and Senior Examiner, GCSE French, Southern
Examining Group

With acknowledgements to Judy Palmer

LONGMAN GROUP UK LIMITED,
Longman House, Burnt Mill, Harlow,
Essex CM20 2JE, England
and Associated Companies throughout the world.

© Longman Group UK Limited 1988
All rights reserved; no part of this publication may be reproduced, stored in a
retrieval system, or transmitted in any form or by any means, electronic,
mechanical, photocopying, recording, or otherwise without either the prior written
permission of the Publishers or a licence permitting restricted copying issued by
the Copyright Licensing Agency Ltd, 33–34 Alfred Place, London, WC1E 7DP.

First published 1988

Set in 10/12 point Helvetica Roman (Linolion)

Produced by Longman Group (F.E.), Limited
Printed in Hong Kong

ISBN 0 582 02453 6

By the same authors
In your own words: French
La boîte aux lettres
Comprenez-vous?
Let's get it right: French
Advanced level essay writing: French
Visa 1 (Students Book, Teachers Book and cassette)
Visa 2 (Students Book, Teachers Book and cassette)
Picture composition French
Talking about pictures: French

In the same series
Role-play practice German
Role-play practice French

Contents

To the teacher

We have written this book in the hope that it will provide much-needed help and guidance to both teachers and pupils in an area of Spanish language learning that is rapidly growing, and likely to grow even more.

There has in particular been a marked shortage of suitable material available for practice, since the Examining Boards have released very little of the material which they have used in examinations. The present book hopes to make good this deficiency. Although the situations included have not themselves been used in examinations, the authors have over twelve years' experience of creating such situations to be used in the oral examinations of the Associated Examining Board and the Southern Examining Group. The level, format and style of the situations are therefore very close to those of the current examinations. It should be stressed, however, that the views expressed in this book are the authors' own, and are in no way an official statement of the policy of any Examining Board or Group.

At the lower level of the GCSE examination there is no real intervention in the role-play by the examiner; such interventions are the rule, however, at the higher levels of the GCSE: we therefore include suggestions for the possible development of each situation along the lines of those provided at present for examiners. These are, however, only suggestions of possibilities, and since role-play is by definition an activity in which it is the pupil who takes the initiative, the possibilities for development are not only endless but impossible to foresee.

In an examination, of course, the candidate does not see the examiner's instructions. For practice purposes, however, there may be much to be gained from pupils seeing how situations are likely to be developed, and indeed the more able pupils should be able to take that part as well, so that situations can be worked out between pairs of pupils.

The above emphasis on the use of such an activity as role-play in examinations should not, however, blind anyone to the fact that, apart from actually visiting Spain, role-playing is the nearest one comes to practising Spanish in a real situation, and this is its prime value: it is a valuable, one might say almost indispensable, rehearsal for real life. But since, for the pupils, doing well in their examinations is also important, it is that aspect we have tended to stress in this book. We hope that both teachers and pupils will find it useful.

TONY WHELPTON
DAPHNE JENKINS

Introduction

Why?

If role-playing appears to be increasing in popularity as far as its inclusion in course-books and examinations is concerned, this is because the learning of foreign languages is increasingly being seen primarily as a means of communication, and the kind of language that is being taught is by and large that which you are most likely to need when visiting the foreign country whose language you are learning.

In other words, it is essentially a matter of rehearsal: of practising for situations which you may very well find yourself having to cope with at some time in the future. Moreover, since when you are abroad you are more likely to be asking questions than answering them, role-play does tend to lay more emphasis on the asking of questions, and the inclusion of role-play in examinations has revealed that this is an area in which traditionally not enough practice has been given.

How to set about it

Let us begin by reminding you of the different ways in which you can ask a simple question.

Imagine that you want to ask a baker if he has any bread rolls:

1   you can change a statement into a question by gestures or facial expressions or by raising your voice at the end, i.e.
        ¿Tiene panecillos?
    Listen carefully to your teacher as he/she pronounces first the statement *Tiene panecillos* and then the question *¿Tiene panecillos?*
2   if the subject is expressed you usually put it after the verb, i.e.
        ¿Tiene Vd panecillos?

3 you can make a statement and change it into a question by
   adding *¿no?* or *¿verdad?* or *¿no es verdad?*, i.e.
       Vd tiene panecillos *¿no?*

Remember that in the written form there will always be an upside
down question mark at the beginning of the question.

What do I have to do?

Whatever the situation in which you find yourself, you will be
required to perform one or more of the following:

1   asking for information
2   giving an explanation
3   asking for something
4   paying for something
5   thanking somebody
6   apologising to somebody
7   complaining about something
8   describing something or someone
9   choosing something
10 expressing an opinion
11 telephoning someone

   You will also, of course, have to go through the usual
exchanges of greeting, farewell and so on, and cope with both
face-to-face and telephone conversations.
   You will find that, although you may be involved in many
different kinds of situation, the number of questions you actually
have to use is comparatively small. You should make sure that
you are familiar with them all, because unless you are, you are
unlikely to be very successful in making yourself understood in
Spain.
   Let us look at each of the above categories, or functions, in turn:

1 Asking for information

Here are some of the more usual questions, words and phrases
that you will need when asking for information. In each case we
have given at least one example of how the item is used in
context.

¿Se puede ... ?
¿Se puede visitar el museo esta mañana?

¿Puedo ... ?
¿Puedo acompañarte al teatro?

¿Puede (Vd) ... ?
¿Puede decirme si hay un buen restaurante por aquí?

¿Hay?
¿Hay un estanco en esta calle?

¿Dónde ... ?
¿Dónde está la piscina?

¿Quiere (Vd) ... ?
¿Quiere firmar aquí?

¿Tiene (Vd) ... ?
¿Tiene algo para el dolor de cabeza?

¿Qué ... ?
¿Qué vas a beber?
¿Qué tipo de flores prefieres?
¿Qué tal?
¿Qué tal la cerveza?

¿Desde cuándo ... ?
¿Desde cuándo vive Vd en Barcelona?

¿Cuánto(s) ... ? ¿Cuánta(s) ... ?
¿Cuánto dinero necesita Vd?
¿Cuántas hermanas tiene?

¿Cuál ... ? ¿Cuáles ... ?
¿Cuál casa prefiere?
¿Cuál de las casas prefiere?
¿Cuál es su ocupación?
¿Cuáles legumbres son las mejores?

¿Cómo ... ?
¿Cómo se dice en español?
No conozco a tu prima. ¿Cómo es?

¿Por qué ... ?
¿Por qué no quieres venir conmigo?

¿Quién . . . ? ¿Quiénes . . . ?
¿Quién toma la sopa?
¿Quiénes prefieren el plato del día?
¿De quién es este libro?

¿Cuándo . . . ?
¿Cuándo llegará el cartero?

¿A qué hora . . . ?
¿A qué hora sale el tren?

Now your turn!

Try using each of the question forms given above in a different situation from the one given, e.g.

¿Se puede comprar periódicos aquí?

2 Giving an explanation

These are some of the most common verbs and structures you will need. We have given examples of how they are used.

Ser
Soy
Soy actor.
Soy inglés.

Estar
Estoy
Estoy en la cocina.
Estoy cansado.

Tener
Tengo
Tengo un hermano y dos hermanas.

Tener que . . .
Tengo que . . .
Tengo que irme mañana.

Deber (de)
Debo (de) . . .
Debo (de) escribir a mi amigo.

Haber
Hay
Hay que hacerlo.

Ir
Voy
Voy al cine esta tarde.

Decidir
He decidido
He decidido ir a Alemania.

Perder
He perdido
He perdido mis gafas.

Necesitar
Necesito
Necesito huevos para cocinar.

Hacer falta
Me hace falta dinero.

Comprender
He comprendido
No he comprendido lo que ha dicho Vd.

Tener miedo
Tengo miedo de mi padre.
Tengo miedo de lastimarme.

Preocuparse
Me preocupa
Me preocupa mucho la enfermedad de mi niño.

Acabar de . . .
Acabo de . . .
Acabo de llegar en España.

Querer
Quiero
Quisiera
Quiero ir a la discoteca.
Quisiera ver a mi novio que es soldado.

Gustar
Me gusta
Me gusta el tenis y me gusta bastante el fútbol.

Encantar
Me encanta
Me encanta esta música.

Parecer
Me parece
Me parece que es verdad.

Now your turn!

Try using each of the verbs given above in a different sentence, e.g.

Mi hermano tiene que acostarse temprano porque tiene solamente cinco años.

3 Asking for something

These are some of the most common verbs and structures, together with examples of how they are used.

Querer
Quiero una habitación doble para una semana.
Quisiera un kilo de peras y un kilo de manzanas.

Desear
Deseo comprar un par de zapatos negros.

Tener ganas de . . .
Tengo ganas de bañarme.

Necesitar
Necesito dos kilos de patatas.

Hacer falta
Me hace falta harina.

Poner
Póngame una botella de vino tinto.

Now your turn!

Try using each of the verbs given above to ask for something different, e.g.

Tengo bastantes legumbres pero hoy necesito peras y naranjas.

4 Paying for something

These are some of the most common verbs and structures, together with examples of their use.

¿Cuánto es?
¿Cuánto es todo?

¿Cuánto vale?
¿Cuánto vale el traje?

¿Cuánto cuesta?
¿Cuánto cuesta la limonada?

Pagar
Pago con mi tarjeta de crédito.

Cobrar
¿Cuánto cobra por hora el ama de casa?

Deber
Le debo cincuenta pesetas.

Tener
Tenga el billete.
Aquí tiene tres billetes.

Tomar
¡Tome! ¡Toma!

Dar
Le doy mil pesetas.

Ser caro
La carne es demasiado cara.

Ser barato
Las legumbres son muy baratas en el mercado.

Now your turn!

Try using each of the verbs and structures given above in a different sentence, e.g.

¿Cuánto vale el vestido con mangas largas?

5 Thanking somebody

These are some of the most common verbs and structures you will need, together with examples of their use.

Gracias
Muchas gracias por la carta.

Dar gracias
Le doy muchas gracias por su amabilidad.

Agradacer
Le agradezco el regalo que me envió.

Estar agradecido
Te estoy muy agradecido.

Ser amable
Es Vd muy amable.

Now your turn!

Practise using these different ways of thanking someone, e.g.

Las rosas son magníficas. Muchísimas gracias.

6 Apologising to somebody

These are some of the most common verbs and structures you will need, together with examples of their use.

Sentir
Lo siento mucho.

Presentar sus excusas
Te presento mis excusas.

Perdonar
Perdóname, me he equivocado.

Pedir perdón
Te pido mil perdones.

Now your turn!

Try apologising to someone using the expressions given above, e.g.

He roto el vaso, madre. Perdóname, te compraré otro.

7 Complaining about something

These are some of the most common verbs and structures you will need, together with examples of their use.

No gustar
No me gusta la lluvia.

No estar contento/satisfecho (de/con)
No estoy contenta de su trabajo.
No estoy satisfecho con mis niños.

Enfadarse
Me he enfadado porque no me has llamado por teléfono.

Estar enfadado/irritado
Estoy enfadado porque la máquina no funciona.
Estoy irritado porque los niños charlan todo el tiempo.

Explicar
¿Quiere Vd explicarme porque la sopa está fría?

Now your turn!

Try using the verbs given above to complain about something, e.g.

El piso no me gusta porque es demasiado pequeño.

8 Describing something or someone

These are the aspects you might need to describe:

Colour
Esto es marrón, azul, blanco, etc.

Esto es verde obscuro.
Esto es verde claro.

Shape
redondo
cuadrado
rectángulo

Size
grande
bastante grande
gordo
enorme
pequeño

Material
de cuero
de algodón
de lana
de nilón

Pattern
sin adornos
a rayas
a (de) cuadros
con puntos

Now your turn!

Use some of the words given above to describe various objects, e.g.

Quisiera un traje gris obscuro a rayas. Prefería tela de lana.

9 Choosing something

These are some of the most common verbs and structures you will need, together with examples of their use.

Tomar
Voy a tomar el plato del día.

Escoger
Escojo el jersey azúl antes que el verde.

Preferir
Prefiero los gatos a los perros.

Gustar
Me gustan más los deportes que la lectura.

Necesitar
Necesito dos sellos.

Valer
Más vale salir que quedarse en casa.

Dar
Deme 250 gramos de jamón.

Poner
Póngame un kilo de habas.

Now your turn!

Try using the verbs given in order to choose something, e.g.

Más vale comprar sellos en el estanco porque no hay correos por aquí.

10   Giving your opinion

These are some of the most common verbs and structures you will need, together with examples of their use.

Creer
Creo que el campo es más tranquilo que la ciudad.
Creo que sí.
Creo que no.

Pensar
Pienso que el libro es muy interesante.
Pienso que sí/no.

Parecer
Me parece que tu novia es muy simpática.

Estar de acuerdo
No estoy de acuerdo.

Estar seguro
Estoy seguro que podré hacerlo.

Ser verdad/cierto
Es verdad/cierto.

Now your turn!

Try using the verbs given above in order to express an opinion, e.g.

Creo que no es verdad lo que has dicho.

11 Telephoning somebody

Here are some phrases which you might meet or need if you are speaking to someone on the telephone:

¡Dígame!
¡Oigame!
¿Me oye(s)?
¡Hola!
Soy yo.
¿Quién habla?
¿De la parte de quién es?
¿Está Pedro?
¿Puedo hablar con María?
Está comunicando.
Se ha confundido de númro.
Hasta luego.

Now your turn!

Try out some of these expressions by holding an imaginary telephone conversation with a friend.

Preparing a role-play situation

Vocabulary

The vocabulary that you will need in role-playing is the basic vocabulary you have learned throughout your course. As you prepare the situations given in this book make sure that you revise all the items that you might want to buy in shops, the food and drink you might order in a restaurant, the information you might require at a travel agency or tourist information office, etc. If there is a particular vocabulary item you don't know, try and find a way of expressing the same idea by using different words.

Playing a part

You must also remember that you will be playing a particular part, and although you do not need to be a great actor or actress, you do need to work out the details of your role. Try and imagine that you really are in a Spanish-speaking country, in the situation you have been given, and ask yourself, "Using the Spanish I know, how can I get this message across?"

Relationship

You must first of all establish what your relationship is with the person to whom you are speaking. If you are speaking to someone you do not know well, or who is older than you, then the relationship will be a formal one, and you must use *usted (Vd)*. But if the other person is a friend, or a member of your family, then the relationship will be an informal one, and you will need to use *tu*. (And if that kind of situation arose in an examination you would probably lose marks for not using *tu*.)

Studying the background information

You must always make sure that you are fully aware of all the details of the situation given to you. You might be told, for example, that you are in a restaurant and have only 700 pesetas to spend. In that case, don't be tempted to spend more money than you have. Likewise, if you are told that you have been waiting for a bus for a long time, don't say that you left home five minutes ago.

Conveying the message

The most important thing to remember about conveying the message in each of the four points you have to get across is that you are not being asked to *translate* from English into Spanish. In fact in an examination, most of the instructions are written in such a way that if you do try and translate them as they stand, you will get into a mess. You must get the basic message across. You will not be asked to say anything which you have not already learnt during your course, and if there is something you don't know, then try and find a way of expressing the ideas in words that you do know.

Often there are several different ways in which you can express the same thing. For example, if you are told to say that you won't forget something again, you might say

No lo olvidaré otra vez.

or

No lo olvidaré nunca más.

or

No volveré a olvidarlo.

You might be told to ask the price of a dress in a shop, in which case you could say either

¿Cuánto es el vestido?

or

¿Cuánto vale el vestido?

or

¿Cuánto cuesta el vestido?

Now your turn!

Find different ways of

1 saying that you won't read the book again
2 asking the price of a green tie.

Developing the situation

If you really were in one of these situations in a Spanish-speaking country, then it is extremely likely that something unexpected might happen. You might find, for instance, that the greengrocer has run out of tomatoes, and asks if you would like something else instead. In an examination you might find the same thing happening, with the examiner intervening in such a way that you have to say something which makes the situation develop. You must think about the possible variations beforehand, and not allow yourself to be taken unawares. If you are booking a room in a hotel, for instance, and you have asked for a room with bath on the first floor, you must be prepared to hear that the only room left is a single room with shower on the ground floor. This, after all, is what tends to happen in real life, so you need to practise coping with it before it does happen.

You must listen very carefully all the time to what the other person is saying, and adapt your own role accordingly. Remember that the other person's intervention is giving you further opportunity to express yourself in Spanish, so always say as much as possible. Never restrict yourself to saying just 'sí' or 'no'. Take the initiative and talk.

In an examination the examiners will have instructions as to how they might try to develop the situation – if the candidates let them! (If the candidates just ignore what the examiners say, then they will lose marks heavily.) In the practice situations given in this book we have given the kind of instructions that the examiner might well have been given for that particular situation; your teacher may want you on occasions to look at that section, or on others to cover it up so that you have to think it out for yourself. If you are preparing for the Basic or General Level of GCSE you will not have to cope with interventions. Nevertheless, it is still good practice for you as you will almost certainly encounter such interventions when you visit a Spanish-speaking country.

Overacting

Talking is not the same thing as acting, and although you are playing a part, you should not feel that you have to act as if you were on stage. By all means put your hand in your pocket and pretend to pay a bill, but do not take it any further than that. Remember that all you have to do is to get your points across, to find out the required information and to adapt your role to the interventions of the other person and the needs of the situation.

Examples of situations

Here are two situations, with an example of how the conversation might possibly go. Obviously, as in real life, someone else might have a totally different conversation based on the same instructions.

Example situation 1

You are in a train, and speak to the person sitting opposite you.

1 Ask whether he/she minds if you open the window.

2 Ask if he/she is going far.

3 Ask if there is a restaurant car on the train.

4 Invite him/her to go with you for a drink.

Fellow passenger

1 Say you don't mind, but it is snowing outside – wouldn't it be better just to turn down the heating?

2 Say you are going to Seville. Where is he/she going? Does he/she live there? It's a long journey, isn't it? Has he/she already eaten?

3 No restaurant car, but a bar which serves drinks.

4 Accept invitation.

How it works

A   ¿Le molesta si abro la ventanilla?

B   No me molesta pero está nevando ¿no? ¿No cree que más vale bajar la calefacción?

A   Me gusta más un poco de aire fresco. ¿Va Vd lejos?

B   Voy a Sevilla. ¿Adónde va Vd?

A   Voy a Cordoba.

B   ¿Vive Vd allí?

A   No, estoy de negocios.

B   Es un viaje muy largo ¿no? ¿Vd ha comido?

A   No. Empiezo a tener hambre. ¿Sabe Vd si hay un coche-restaurante en este tren?

B   No hay uno, pero hay un bar donde se sirven bebidas.

A   Bueno. ¿Tiene Vd sed? ¿Quiere venir beber conmigo?

B   Con mucho gusto. ¡Qué buen idea! ¡Vámonos!

Example situation 2

You are at home, and telephone a Spanish friend called Miguel. Miguel's brother answers the phone, and tells you that Miguel is out.

1   Ask when he will be back.

2   Ask if he received your letter this morning.

3   Ask if he has decided to go out with you this evening.

4   Say you have tickets for a concert and ask if Miguel will ring you when he comes in.

Miguel's brother

1   Say he has gone to the library, and you don't know when he will be back. Can you take a message?

2   Say you don't think he got a letter today. When was it posted?

3   Say you know he intends to go out this evening, but you don't know who with. Where is he/she thinking of going?

4   Ask for his/her telephone number and if he/she will be at home all afternoon.

How it works

A ¿Cuándo va a regresar a casa?

B Ha ido a la biblioteca y no sé cuando va a regresar. ¿Quieres darme un recado?

A Sí, por favor. ¿Sabes si recibió mi carta esta mañana?

B Creo que no. ¿Cuándo la echaste al correos?

A Ayer por la mañana a eso de las diez.

B Pues, llegará a la mejor esta tarde.

A Bueno. ¿Quisiera saber si él ha decidido salir conmigo esta tarde?

B Yo sé que tiene la intención de salir pero no me ha dicho con quien. ¿Adónde quieres ir?

A Tengo dos billetes para un concierto y quisiera ir allí con Miguel. ¿Quieres pedirle que me llame cuando esté de vuelta?

B Por supuesto. ¿Qué es tu número de teléfono?

A El 24 16 83.

B El 24 16 83. Bueno. ¿Estarás en casa toda la tarde?

A Sí. Esperaré su llamada.

B Se lo diré.

A Muchas gracias. Adiós.

B Adiós.

Shopping

Situation 1

You go into a *panadería*, and speak to the shopkeeper.

1   Ask for two loaves of bread.

2   Ask for six bread rolls.

3   Ask how much the little cake in the window is, and buy it.

4   Ask how much it all comes to, and offer a 500-peseta note.

Vocabulary

Un pan
Una barra de pan
Un panecillo
Un pastel
El escaparate
Un billete de 500 pesetas
¿Cuánto vale?
¿Cuánto es todo?
La moneda

Shopkeeper

1 Ask what kind of loaves.

2 Say there are none left. Would he/she like something else instead?

3 Say the cake is 135 pesetas.

4 Say how much it costs and ask if he/she has any change. (Cost is 315 pesetas.)

Situation 2

You go into a *pastelería*, and speak to the shop assistant.

1 Say you would like a cake; ask which he/she recommends.

2 Ask how much the coffee cake and the cream cakes are.

3 Say the cream cakes are too expensive.

4 Say you do not like chocolate cakes and buy a coffee cake.

Vocabulary

Recomendar
Una ensaimada
Un pastel de nata
Un pastel de chocolate
Gustar

Shop assistant

1 The coffee cake is 150 pesetas and the cream cakes 80 pesetas each.

2 Say the chocolate cakes are not so expensive.

3 The coffee cake is very good and not too expensive.

4 Offer other cakes (tortas, tartas, etc.).

Situation 3

You are out shopping and you go into a *tienda de ultramarinos*. You speak to the shopkeeper.

1 Ask how much the ham costs, and when he/she has told you, buy 250 grams.

2 Ask which sausage he/she recommends, and buy half a kilo.

3 Order a roast chicken for tomorrow.

4 Apologise for only having a 500-peseta note.

Vocabulary

El jamón
El jamón serrano
La salchicha
El chorizo
El salchichón
Un medio kilo
Mañana
Un pollo asado

Shopkeeper

1 Say the *jamón de York* is 600 pesetas a kilo, but the *serrano* is better. When asked, say it is 670 pesetas a kilo.

2 Suggest *chorizo* or *salchichón*. Recommend the *chorizo* that you have just made, at 480 pesetas a kilo.

3 What weight of chicken? (From 2 to 4 kilos). When will he/she come to collect it?

4 Say the bill (without chicken) comes to 407 pesetas.

Situation 4

You are in a clothes shop in Spain. You have seen a dress (or a shirt) in the shop window, but you cannot see it in the shop. You have a maximum of 3500 pesetas to spend. You speak to a sales assistant.

1 Ask about the dress (or the shirt).

2 Ask if you can try it on.

3 Ask if he/she has any belts (or ties) to go with it.

4 Say you prefer one of the belts (or ties) and ask how much it is.

Vocabulary

Un vestido
Una camisa
Probar
Una corbata
Un cinturón
Hacer juego
Ser a tono

Sales assistant

1   Ask for exact details of the dress (or shirt).
    Say it costs 2500 pesetas.

2   Would he/she like to try on something else as well? Ask
    his/her opinion of other items.

3   What kind of belt (leather, synthetic, wide/narrow, colour, etc.)
    or tie (material, colour, stripes, etc.)?

4   It is 600 pesetas, but you have a better one for 750 pesetas.

    Ask if he/she wishes to buy.

Situation 5

You go into a clothes shop. You have just bought a new jacket and want to buy matching garments. You speak to the sales assistant.

1 Say you want to buy a shirt (or blouse) to match your new jacket and buy one of those offered.

2 Say you also need a tie (or jumper) and choose one of those offered.

3 Ask if they have any nylon socks (or woollen gloves) and buy two pairs.

4 Ask if they accept cheques or a credit card.

Vocabulary

Una chaqueta
Una blusa
Un jersey
Los calcetines
de nilón
de lana
Los guantes
Un par
Una tarjeta de crédito
Un cheque

Sales assistant

1 Ask the colour and what the jacket is made of, and offer two shirts/blouses, one at 1800, one at 2200 pesetas.

2 Offer choice of ties at 600 pesetas each or jumpers at 1600 or 2000 pesetas.

3 Ask what colour socks or gloves and whether plain or patterned. Offer them at 258 pesetas a pair (socks) and 420 pesetas a pair (gloves).

4 Present bill and accept cheque or credit card. Bill will range from 2916 pesetas to 5000 pesetas, depending on items chosen.

Situation 6

You are a Spanish man or woman, el Señor Vega/la Señora Vega. You are in a Spanish market, and go to the stall of a greengrocer you know quite well.

1   Ask how he/she is, and ask about his/her family.

2   Say you want some large onions.

3   Ask for a cauliflower and a cabbage.

4   Buy a kilo of apples.

Vocabulary

La familia
Una cebolla
Un coliflor
Un col
Una manzana

Greengrocer

1 Ask how he/she likes his/her new job. Does he/she have to travel a lot?

2 Are these onions large enough? Recommend some cheaper ones.

3 Offer various sizes and prices. Say the cabbages are not very fresh, but you are expecting some more later on.

   Ask if he/she would like some fruit today.

4 Tell him/her the price: about 360 pesetas to 400 pesetas, depending on what he/she has bought.

Situation 7

You are in a supermarket and see a man drop a purse. You try to catch him but he goes out of the shop before you can do so. You look inside the purse and then go to see the manager.

1 Say you saw a man drop the purse.

2 Say that you have opened the purse but there is no name or address in it.

3 Describe the contents of the purse.

4 Ask what the manager will do if the man doesn't claim the purse.

Vocabulary

El bolso
Dejar caer
El apellido
La dirección
Contener
El gerente
Reclamar
Devolver

Manager

1 Ask why he/she didn't give it back to the man.

2 Ask what the man was like.

3 Ask what is in the purse.

4 Say you will give it to the police, but ask for his/her name and address.

Situation 8

You are visiting some friends for lunch and you want to buy some flowers for your hostess. You go to a florist's shop. You do not want to spend more than 400 pesetas.

1   Say you want to buy some flowers.

2   Ask the florist for some advice.

3   Find out the prices and choose some flowers.

4   Buy the flowers, then ask the way to the nearest metro station.

Vocabulary

La flor
Aconsejar
Un ramo
Una docena
Una rosa
Un clavel
Una estación de metro
Una parada de autobús

Florist

1 Is it for a present? For someone special?

2 Suggest roses or carnations.

3 Large roses are 440 pesetas a bunch, smaller ones
  300 pesetas. Carnations are 180 pesetas a dozen.

  If roses chosen, ask which colour.

4 It is quite a long way, but there is a bus stop opposite.
  Where is he/she going?

  The number 10 bus stops near there.

Situation 9

You have arranged to meet a friend outside a big department store in a Spanish town, but arrive early, so you look around the shop. You go to the information desk and speak to a shop assistant.

1 Ask where the toy department is.

2 Ask if you can get there by lift.

3 Ask if there is a café in the shop and if lunch is served there.

4 Ask at what time the shop usually shuts and if there is an evening when it stays open late.

Vocabulary

El departamento de juguetes
El ascensor
En el tercer piso
No funcionar
Una cafetería

Copies

Shop assistant

1   Say that it is on the fourth floor and that there is an excellent choice. What is he/she looking for?

2   Yes, but the lift is out of order. Suggest escalator or stairs.

3   The main café is on the top floor; lunch will be over now, but there is a snack bar on the first floor. Will that do? What does he/she want to eat?

4   The shop usually shuts at 8.30 p.m. and there is no late evening shopping. Does he/she know the supermarket in the same street? It stays open until 10 p.m. several evenings a week.

Situation 10

You are staying in a Spanish town and you are out shopping. Soon after coming out of a large store you realise that you no longer have your wallet/handbag. You go back into the shop and ask to speak to the manager.

1   Apologise for bothering him/her.

2   Tell him/her about losing your wallet/handbag.

3   Ask what you should do.

4   Ask if he/she thinks there is a chance that it might be found.

Vocabulary

La cartera
La bolsa
Molestar
El dependiente/La dependienta
La comisaría de policía

Manager

1 Say it doesn't matter and ask how you can help.

2 Exactly when and where was the handbag/wallet lost? Which assistant was helping him/her at the time? Has he/she spoken to this assistant about the loss?

Ask what was in the wallet/handbag.

3 Suggest that he/she reports it to the nearest police station.

Does he/she know where that is? Give directions.

4 Yes, there is a chance somebody might return it to your office, but there are a lot of thieves about. Does he/she think it might have been stolen, or did he/she drop it?

Suggest he/she comes back the next day.

Situation 11

You go into a grocer's shop, and speak to the grocer.

1 Ask for 100 grams of ham and a tin of sardines.

2 Say you would like some cheese.

3 Ask him/her to recommend some good wine. Buy two bottles and also a bottle of fizzy mineral water.

4 Choose a packet of biscuits and a bar of chocolate.

Vocabulary

Cien gramos
Una lata de sardinas
El queso
El vino
Una botella
El agua mineral con gas
Un paquete
Una galleta
Una barra de chocolate

Grocer

1   Boiled ham or country ham? Portuguese or French sardines?

2   Ask what kind of cheese he/she prefers (hard, soft, cream, blue, etc.).

3   What is the wine to go with? Make appropriate suggestions. Wine costs 160, 180 and 320 pesetas.

4   Recommend various kinds of biscuits and chocolate. Is that everything? Ask for payment.

Situation 12

You go into a greengrocer's shop in Spain, but you do not have much money, and you must buy the cheapest fruit and vegetables. You speak to the greengrocer.

1   Buy some carrots and a kilo of onions.

2   Ask for the greengrocer's advice on other vegetables.

3   Ask about peaches and pears and decide which fruit to buy.

4   Ask for half a kilo of white grapes.

Vocabulary

Las legumbres
Las zanahorias
Las uvas blancas
Los tomates
Los guisantes
Los melocotones
Las mandarinas
Las peras

Greengrocer

1 Large or small carrots? Large are 50 pesetas, small are 30 pesetas. Large onions are 35 pesetas, small are 25 pesetas.

2 Tomatoes are good value at 75 pesetas a kilo and peas at 60 pesetas.

3 Peaches are 65 pesetas a kilo, pears 75 pesetas. Suggest tangerines at 55 pesetas a kilo.

4 No grapes at present; they will arrive later. Would he/she like to come back?

Ask if he/she would like something else. Ask for payment.

Situation 13

You go into a shop and speak to a shop assistant.

1 Say you were in the shop earlier, and think you left an umbrella behind.

2 Say it was blue and white and not very long.

3 Describe the assistant who served you.

4 Ask if they will let you know if they find it.

Vocabulary

Temprano
Un paraguas
Olvidar
Servir
Avisar
El número de teléfono
Encontrar

Shop assistant

1 Ask what time he/she was in the shop.

2 Ask who it was who served him/her.

3 Ask if he/she remembers exactly where the umbrella was left.

4 Ask for name, address and telephone number.

Situation 14

You are staying in Madrid and have been involved in a slight accident. A jacket (or a dress) that you want to wear this evening has been slightly torn and needs cleaning. You go to a dry cleaner's, and speak to a shop assistant.

1 Say you want the jacket/dress cleaned.

2 Find out when it will be ready.

3 Ask if it can be repaired as well.

4 Ask if it can be delivered to your hotel when it is ready.

Vocabulary

Limpiar (en seco)
Listo
Reparar
Entregar
La mancha
Un pago adicional
Rasgar
Urgente

Shop assistant

1   Find out what the stains are and what caused them.

2   It will be ready in two days' time.

It can only be ready today with extra payment, and even then it might not be ready. But let yourself be persuaded.

3   You do repairs, but clothes have to be sent away, so it won't be back for a few days. The tear is not very serious: suggest that he/she could repair it.

4   You do not normally deliver. Why is it so urgent?

What time is it needed? Which hotel? As it is so near you can deliver it when you leave work.

Situation 15

You go into a dry cleaner's shop in Spain, and speak to the assistant.

1   Ask to have your dress/trousers cleaned.

2   Ask when it/they will be ready as you will be leaving the next day.

3   Ask how much it will cost.

4   Ask if clothes can be delivered to your hotel as you will be out all day.

Vocabulary

El servicio ordinario
El servicio expreso
El pantalón
Verter
Marcharse/Irse
Entregar

54

Assistant

1 Ask what has been spilt on it/them.

2 Explain that the ordinary service takes two days, but there is an express service that takes two hours.

3 The ordinary service is 360 pesetas. The express service is 520 pesetas. Which will he/she have?

4 Ask which hotel he/she is staying at.
Suggest he/she calls just before closing-time (8.30 p.m.) or early next morning (shop opens at 8 a.m.)

In the restaurant

Situation 16

You are in a restaurant with a friend.

1   Ask your friend if he/she has decided what to eat.

2   Ask what kind of wine he/she would prefer.

3   Ask if he/she has been to this place before.

4   Ask what he/she would like to do later on.

Vocabulary

Ir a tomar
Escoger
La comida
El vino de casa
El cine
La película
El teatro
El concierto

Friend

1 Say you are not sure. What does he/she think?

   Say you don't like what is suggested and suggest something else.

2 Will the house wine do, as the other wines are rather expensive?

3 Say you haven't been here before. Has he/she? If yes, was the food good? If not, how did he/she come to hear of it?

4 Would he/she like to go to the cinema? If yes, what kind of film does he/she prefer? If no, what about the theatre or a concert?

Copied

Situation 17

You go into a restaurant with a friend who does not speak Spanish. You do not want to spend more than 1000 pesetas each. You speak to the waiter.

1   Ask if there is a free table.

2   Ask for the menu and for the waiter's advice.

3   Say that that is too expensive and ask how much chicken and chips would cost.

4   Ask waiter to recommend wine.

Vocabulary

Una mesa libre
El menú
El pollo
Las patatas fritas
El plato principal

Cored

Waiter

1 Ask for how many people and where they would like to sit.

2 Recommend the *steak a la pimienta*. It costs 1000 pesetas each.

3 Chicken and chips is 750 pesetas each.

   Ask if they would like an *entremés* before their main course.

4 Suggest a Valdepeñas at 400 pesetas a bottle, or *vino de casa* at 160 pesetas.

   Ask if they would like an *aperitivo*.

Situation 18

You are in a restaurant in Spain with a friend who does not speak Spanish, so you must order for him/her as well as for yourself. You do not want to spend more than 2400 pesetas in all. You speak to the waiter/waitress.

1 Ask if there is a menu for tourists.

2 Find out what choice is offered for the cheapest meal.

3 Ask if wine is included and order some.

4 Ask if you will have to wait long, as you are in a hurry.

Vocabulary

El menú del día
El menú turístico
La comida más barata
Incluido
La carta de vinos
Una jarra de vino
Tener prisa

Waiter/waitress

1 There is a set meal at 1500 pesetas and a tourist menu at 1200 pesetas.

2 There is a choice of *tortilla*, *pollo asado* or *chuleta de cordero*.

Ask which vegetables they would like.

3 Service is included, but not wine.

Say the house wine is very good, and give them a wine list.

Ask which *entremés* they would like. (*Sopa, melón* or *ensalada mixta*.)

4 Say you will serve them straight away.

Situation 19

You are in a restaurant in Spain with a friend who does not speak Spanish. Neither of you has enjoyed the meal and you send for the manager to express your dissatisfaction.

1 Complain about the meat not being properly cooked.

2 The service was poor; you had to wait too long between courses.

3 The waiter forgot to bring the glass of water you had asked for.

4 There is a mistake in the bill.

Vocabulary

Bien cocido
Esperar
El plato
El camarero
Olvidar
Traer
Pedir
Un vaso de agua
Un error
La cuenta

Manager

1 Find out what was ordered and what instructions given.

2 Explain that the waiter is new. Did they tell him they were in a hurry?

3 Apologise about water. Would they like a drink now?

4 Identify the error: say the waiter is not used to their prices. Apologise and change bill. Promise better service in future.

Situation 20

You are on holiday in Spain, but you are the only one in your party who can speak Spanish. You go into a restaurant and speak to the waiter.

1   Ask if they have a table free.

2   Try and get a table on the terrace overlooking the garden.

3   Order the set meal for everyone.

4   Ask the waiter what he recommends.

Vocabulary

La terraza
Tener vista a
Hacer fresco
Fuera
Dentro
El comedor
El postre

Waiter

1 Ask how many in the party and where they would like to sit.

2 Say there is one table left on the terrace but it is rather cool outside. Would they prefer an inside table?

3 Say there are two set meals. Which one would they like?

4 Ask which starter, main course, vegetables and dessert they would like.

At the hotel

Situation 21

You have just arrived at a hotel in Spain with your parents and your brother who do not speak Spanish. You speak to the hotel receptionist.

1 Say you want two rooms for one night.

2 Say you would like rooms which look on to the garden and which are near one another.

3 Ask the price of the rooms including breakfast.

4 Ask what time breakfast is served and if you can have it in the bedroom.

Vocabulary

El recepcionista
Dar al jardín
Una habitación doble
Una habitación individual
Con baño
Cercano
El piso principal
El primer piso

Receptionist

1 For how many people? With bath?

2 Offer one on the ground floor and one on the second floor.
  Say there are two together on the first floor but only one looks
  on to garden.

3 The rooms are 1130 pesetas each. Breakfast is 160 pesetas
  extra.

4 Breakfast is 7.30 to 9.15 a.m. Will they be leaving early?

Situation 22

You are on holiday in Spain with your family, consisting of father, mother, a 16-year-old girl and her twin brother. You may play the part of any member of the family that you choose, but you are the only one who speaks Spanish. You go into a hotel and speak to the receptionist.

1 Ask if you can have some rooms.

2 You would prefer rooms with a good view, and not too close to the kitchen.

3 Decide whether to accept what you are offered, and ask if you can have dinner in the hotel.

4 Ask if there is a lift and if you can have help with your luggage.

Vocabulary

Una vista
El equipaje
El mozo

Receptionist

1 Ask what he/she requires. How many people/rooms? Other requirements (bath/shower)?

2 You have one room on the ground floor (not close to kitchen), and two on the second floor.

3 Dinner is available: what time would they like to eat? Would they like breakfast in their rooms in the morning? At what time?

4 There is a lift. The porter will help. Where is the luggage?

Situation 23

You are staying in a hotel in Spain and you are the only member of your family who can speak Spanish. Your young brother/sister has been ill during the night. The following morning you speak to the receptionist.

1 Explain the problem.

2 Ask about local doctors.

3 Ask about possibility of changing rooms because of traffic noise.

4 Ask about possibility of providing meals in bedroom.

Vocabulary

Ponerse enfermo/Sentirse mal
Tener fiebre
El médico
Cambiar de habitación
El ruido
El tráfico
Llamar al médico
El consultorio
Las horas de consulta

Receptionist

1 Express concern and enquire about illness (was it sudden, possible causes, etc.).

2 Suggest names of doctors. Is boy/girl fit to go to surgery? If so, give times. If not, offer to ask doctor to visit.

3 Say the only room available is on the top floor. Will that do, or will they wait until the next day?

4 Usually only serve breakfast in bedrooms, but can take up lunch and dinner. For mother and father too? What would the patient/they like to eat?

On the telephone

Situation 24

You are at home and telephone a Spanish friend who has been ill.

1 Ask what has been the matter and if he/she is better.

2 Ask if he/she is able to get up now.

3 Ask if there is anything you can do to help.

4 Ask if he/she would like some fruit – grapes or oranges.

Vocabulary

¿Qué has tenido?
Estar mejor
Ayudar
La naranja
Descansar
Una revista
La gripe

Friend

1   Say you have had 'flu, but are feeling much better now.

Ask if he/she will come and see you as you can't go out for a few days.

2   You can get up, but you have to rest a lot.

3   Ask him/her to bring you a magazine that you like.

4   You don't feel much like eating fruit, but you would like something to drink.

Situation 25

You telephone a Spanish friend.

1 Apologise for not having turned up to meet him/her yesterday.

2 Suggest meeting on Saturday.

3 Would he/she like to go with you to a party at a friend's house?

4 Arrange details of meeting.

Vocabulary

Ayer
Una fiesta
Encontrarse
Prestar

Friend

1 Ask what happened.

   Why didn't he/she telephone before?

2 Saturday is difficult. You have a lot to do. What is he/she
   thinking of doing?

3 Ask for details (when, where, dress, etc.).

4 Agree to go.

   You might be able to borrow your father's car. Would he/she
   like a lift?

Situation 26

**You have been staying in Madrid but have not been well, and
this has prevented you from getting in touch with a friend
whom you had promised to contact. You now telephone
him/her.**

1 Apologise and explain why you have not been in touch.

2 Suggest a meeting: give time and place.

3 Suggest where you can go together.

4 You need to buy a good Spanish dictionary, but you do not
   know where to go to buy it.

Vocabulary

Juntos – as
Estar malo
Llamar por teléfono
Citarse
Un diccionario
Un abrigo
La librería

Friend

1 Accept apology and ask how he/she is now.

2 You would like to meet but time and place not suitable.
  Suggest alternative and make arrangements.

3 You need to buy a new coat; will he/she help you choose?

4 Suggest a Velazquez dictionary and one of the bookshops in
  the Calle de Atocha. Say you will take him/her there. Suggest
  having a meal together: time depending on arrangements
  already made. Discuss kind of restaurant you might go to.

Situation 27

You are staying in a Spanish town and you telephone a Spanish friend.

1 Suggest that you meet.

2 Invite him/her out to a meal.

3 Ask him/her to recommend a good restaurant.

4 Choose one of the places recommended and arrange meeting.

Vocabulary

Invitar
Encantado
Francés

Friend

1   You would be delighted, but when and where?

2   Accept, but you are not free on day suggested. Suggest another day.

    Ask whether it is for lunch or dinner.

3   What kind of restaurant has he/she in mind (large, small, Spanish, French)?

    Recommend several restaurants in the town centre.

4   Ask exactly where he/she is staying.

    Suggest either meeting in front of the Post Office or collecting him/her in your car.

Situation 28

It is your birthday and you have received a present of a blouse (or a shirt) from a Spanish friend. You telephone your friend.

1 Express your thanks.

2 Say what you are doing to celebrate your birthday.

3 Ask if you can go and stay with him/her during the summer holidays.

4 Ask about the health of other members of the family.

Vocabulary

El cumpleaños
¡Feliz cumpleaños!
Celebrar
El regalo
Las vacaciones de verano
Ir bien (= to suit) (Eso te va bien)

Friend

1 Wish him/her a happy birthday.

Ask if he/she likes the colour, and if the shirt/blouse suits him/her.

2 Ask what other presents he/she has had.

3 Ask when he/she wants to come and for how long. Explain your own holiday plans.

4 Say they are all well, but your sister is tired as she is working very hard for her exams. Ask about his/her family. Ask why he/she hasn't written recently.

Situation 29

You are in a Spanish town on your way to stay with some friends. Unfortunately your plane was late arriving, and you have missed the last train to the small town where your friends live. You telephone your friends.

1 Ask if anyone has gone to meet you at the station yet.

2 Explain what has happened and apologise for being late.

3 Ask what you should do next.

4 Say you will catch a train the following morning.

Vocabulary

Estar para salir
Ir al encuentro de
Coger un tren
El vuelo
Llegar tarde
Enfrente de

Friend

1   You were just about to get the car out of the garage. Where is he/she phoning from?

2   Ask why the flight was delayed.

3   When is the next train?

Has he/she enough money to stay in a hotel?
If yes, try the large hotel opposite the station.
If no, would he/she like you to come by car to pick him/her up?

4   Does he/she know times of trains the next morning?
Has he/she had a meal? If not, suggest he/she has something to eat.

Situation 30

You are telephoning a friend who lives in Madrid.

1 Say you are coming to Madrid for a few days and would like to see him/her.

2 Ask how far your hotel in the Calle de Alcalá is from your friend's house.

3 Suggest that you visit a museum together.

4 Ask about getting to this meeting by bus or metro.

Vocabulary

La semana que viene
Un museo
En autobús
En el metro

Friend

1   Say you would love to, but will be working all day, so which
    day will he/she be free in the evening?
    Invite him/her to dinner one evening.

2   Offer to go and fetch him/her by car.

3   Ask what he/she would like to see most, and suggest museum
    accordingly.

4   If bus, suggest metro might be quicker and cheaper. If metro,
    suggest bus might be more interesting.

    Ask time and place of meeting.

At the garage

Situation 31

You are in your parents' car in Spain, but your parents cannot speak Spanish. You stop at a petrol station, and speak to the petrol pump attendant.

1 Ask for some petrol, and ask him/her to check the oil and the tyre pressure.

2 Ask how far it is to the nearest town.

3 Ask if you can buy cigarettes and sweets here.

4 Ask how much it is, and if you can pay by credit card.

Vocabulary

La gasolina
Super
Normal
Llenar el depósito
Comprobar
El nivel
El aceite
Un medio litro
La presión
El neumático
Los dulces
La tarjeta de crédito

Pump attendant

1 Ask what kind of petrol and how much.

  Tell him/her that the car needs half a litre of oil, but the tyres don't need any air.

2 It is about 20 km, but if they are looking for somewhere to have lunch, there is a good restaurant in a village about 5 km away.

3 Say yes, and ask what he/she would like.

4 Work out price at 60 pesetas a litre and 120 pesetas for oil, plus cigarettes and sweets.

Situation 32

You are on a motoring holiday in Spain, but are the only one in the party to speak Spanish. You go to a petrol station, and speak to a petrol pump attendant.

1 Buy petrol and get oil checked.

2 Ask where the toilet is.

3 Ask if one can buy sweets and drinks for the children.

4 Ask what there is to see and do in the nearest town.

Vocabulary

Los servicios
Al fondo
Una bebida
El pueblo más cercano
Un edificio
La equitación
La natación
La piscina

Pump attendant

1 Ask how much petrol and what kind.

2 The toilet is at the back: first door on the left.

3 Say there are no hot drinks; what cold drinks would they like?

There are no sweets left; they will have to go to the nearest town for sweets.

4 What kind of places do they like to visit? Depending on answer, suggest: old buildings, churches, market place, etc.

What kind of activities do they prefer? Depending on answer, suggest: swimming pool, park, horse-riding, etc.

Ask where they come from and how long they are staying. If necessary, ask to be paid for petrol and drinks.

In the street

Situation 33

You have witnessed an accident, and you approach a policeman who has just arrived.

1　Say it was you who telephoned the police.

2　Tell him that you saw what happened.

3　Say that you were standing at the bus stop when a little boy ran out in the road in front of a car.

4　Say that you shouted to try and stop him.

Vocabulary

Telefonear a la policía
Lo que pasó
La parada de autobús
Delante
Gritar
Impedir
Una llamada

Policeman

1 Ask his/her name and address.

2 Ask what happened.

3 Ask why the car did not stop more quickly.

4 Say if he/she knows the little boy and where he lives.

 Thank him/her and ask for telephone number. Ask when he/she will be at home to receive a call.

Situation 34

You are in town, and see a friend whom you have not seen for some time. You go over and speak to him/her.

1 Ask how he/she is, and how his/her family are.

2 Ask why he/she hasn't been to see you for so long.

3 Suggest meeting soon.

4 Ask if he/she has time to come and have a quick drink with you now.

Vocabulary

Ocupado
Tomar unas copas
Tener tiempo para

Friend

1 Say you are all well; what about his/her family?

2 Say you have been very busy with your new job. Why didn't he/she phone?

3 Accept, but where and when? Make suggestions if necessary (e.g. cinema, café).

4 Accept, but ask where you can go, as you haven't much time to spare.

Situation 35

You have just arrived in Spain on holiday when your car breaks down about 50 km from the coast. Another motorist stops, and you go and speak to him/her.

1   Say that you have broken down, but you don't know what is wrong.

2   Ask for help in changing the wheel as you have never done it before.

3   Ask if he/she knows a good restaurant nearby.

4   Thank him/her for helping, and offer to take him/her to a café for a drink.

Vocabulary

Averiar(se)
Lo que no marcha
Cambiar de rueda
Un pinchazo
El neumático de atrás
El neumático de recambio
Las herramientas

Motorist

1 Say you think there is a puncture in one of the rear tyres.

2 Ask where the spare tyre and the tools are kept.

3 Say there is a good restaurant called 'Los Arcos' in the next village, about 2 km further on.

   Ask how much further he/she has to drive today.

4 Say you live nearby, and invite him/her to your house for a drink instead.

Situation 36

You are in Barcelona, and you want to go to the Plaza Bonanova. You are on foot, and you ask a passer-by for advice.

1   You ask the best way to get there: on foot or by bus?

2   Ask how long it will take.

3   Choose a means of transport and ask for directions.

4   Repeat the directions. Say thank you, and ask if there is a bank in the Plaza Bonanova.

Vocabulary

A pie
La librería
El banco
La parada de taxis

Passer-by

1 Say it depends whether he/she is in a hurry. It is quite a long walk, and the bus has just gone. Suggest taxi.

2 Ten minutes by taxi, longer if he/she waits for next bus or walks.

3 If bus: bus stop is opposite book shop just down the road. If taxi: taxi rank is first left, then second right.

   All taxis are painted yellow and black.

4 Say you are sure there are several banks there. Which one does he/she want?

Situation 37

You are staying in Madrid and have arranged to visit a friend who lives near the University. You have been waiting for a bus for a long time, but no bus has come. You approach a passer-by, and engage him/her in conversation.

1 Ask why there are no buses.

2 You are in a hurry. Ask how else you can get there.

3 Find out where the nearest phone box is so that you can ring your friend.

4 You do not know your friend's phone number. How can you find out?

Vocabulary

Estar en huelga
La cabina telefónica
La guía telefónica

Passer-by

1 The buses are on strike today. How long has he/she been waiting?

2 Suggest taxi or metro, but the metro station is rather a long way away.

Find out exactly where he/she is going and what time he/she is due to arrive there.

3 There is no phone box in this street, but he/she could try the nearby café.

4 Ascertain if he/she knows name and address of friend. Tell him/her to look in phone directory or ask someone in café to help.

At the railway station

Situation 38

You are on your way to stay with a Spanish family in a small Spanish town. You have just arrived at the railway station, and there is no-one there to meet you. You telephone the family and one of your friend's parents answers the phone.

1   Say you have just arrived at the station.

2   You caught the 8 o'clock train as your plane arrived earlier than expected.

3   You tried to ring from the airport, but no one answered.

4   How do you get to their house?

Vocabulary

Acabar de (+ Infinitive)
Más temprano
Ir de compras
Reconocer
Llevar

Father/mother

1 Express surprise at early arrival and ask for an explanation.

2 Why hadn't he/she let you know?

3 Nobody answered as you had all gone shopping.

4 Say you will come and fetch him/her in the car. How will you be able to recognise him/her? What is he/she wearing?

   Where will you find him/her?

   Did he/she have a good journey?

   What has he/she had to eat? Would he/she like to go into the cafeteria to have a drink as it will take you a quarter of an hour to get there.

Situation 39

You are at the taxi rank at a railway station in a Spanish town. You have a lot of luggage, and want to go to the airport to catch the 9.30 a.m. plane to London. You speak to a taxi-driver.

1   Ask the taxi-driver if he is free.

2   Say you haven't much time to spare, and how long will it take?

3   Ask him to help you with your luggage.

4   Say you have to be in London before lunch in order to meet your parents.

Vocabulary

Un taxista
El aeropuerto
Londres
La maleta
Pertenecer

Taxi-driver

1 Say yes and ask where he/she wants to go.

2 Say it depends on the traffic, but you usually do it in about half an hour.

Ask what time is the flight.

3 Ask which suitcases belong to him/her.

Comment on weight of cases, and ask how long he/she has been staying in Spain.

4 Ask if there is another flight that morning.

Say you will do your best to arrive in time.

At the travel agency

Situation 40

You are a Spaniard. You are in a Spanish town and you want to visit friends in a town 50 km away, with your children aged nine and three. You visit a travel agency to enquire about the journey and, if possible, to buy tickets. You speak to the travel agent.

1 Ask if it is possible to travel by train.

  If it is, ask if you need to change trains, and if there is an alternative means of transport.

2 Ask how long the journey will take, and about departure times.

3 Ask how much it will cost and buy your tickets.

Vocabulary

En tren
Viajar
Cambiar de tren
El modo de transporte
Las horas de salida
Un billete de ida solamente
Un billete de ida y vuelta
Media tarifa

Travel agent

1   Say it is possible, but there is no direct service.

Say there is a direct coach service. Which would he/she prefer?

2   By train it takes four hours. There are several trains a day, but you have to change at Madrid.

By coach it takes six hours, but there is only one coach a day, and it leaves at 10 a.m.

3   Ask how many travelling, and age of children. Single or return?

If train, under four travel free. First or second class?
Fares: first class 2400 pesetas single, second class 1700 pesetas. Return is double, children pay half.
If coach, fares: 1400 pesetas single. Return double, children over three pay half.

Does he/she want to buy tickets now? Arrange payment.

Situation 41

You are spending your summer holiday in a Spanish town, 100 km from the coast. You decide you would like to spend a few days at the seaside. You go to a travel agency to make enquiries, and speak to the travel agent.

1 Ask which are the best seaside resorts within easy reach.

2 Ask about different kinds of accommodation there.

3 Ask about the cheapest and quickest way of getting there.

4 Make arrangements for your journey.

Vocabulary

Un punto de veraneo
El alojamiento
Una playa de arena
Un parador
Una pensión
Un albergue

Travel agent

1 Does he/she want a large sandy beach or an interesting town?

2 Does he/she want a hotel, *parador*, *albergue*, *pensión* or *camping*? Depending on which chosen, ask for more detailed requirements: number in party, length of stay, etc., and offer to book.

3 Train is fast and direct. Coach is cheaper but slower.

4 What day and time does he/she want to travel?

At the tourist information office

Situation 42

You have just arrived in a Spanish town, and you go to the *Oficina de turismo* for information. You speak to an employee.

1   Ask for help in finding a hotel.

2   Ask what there is to do and see in the region.

3   Ask if there is a restaurant in the hotel and whether there are good restaurants in the town.

4   Ask if there is a cinema in the town.

Vocabulary

La región
El confort
La duración
La visita/La estancia

Employee

1 Ask what kind of hotel: price, comfort, length of stay, number in party.

 Recommend Hotel San Isidro.

2 Ask what he/she is interested in, then suggest anything suitable – museum, swimming, etc.

3 Offer a list of restaurants in the town.

4 Say there is no cinema here, only in the next town, which is 6 km away. Has he/she a car? If not, there are plenty of buses.

 Wish him/her a good stay.

Situation 43

You are visiting Spain with your family: you have a young child, and do not want too expensive a holiday. On arriving at a seaside town you go to the *Oficina de turismo* and speak to an employee.

1 Ask if you can have a plan of the town.

2 Ask for a list of hotels and some advice about the best places to stay.

3 Ask where the best shops are, and where the best restaurants are.

4 Ask about interesting places to visit and things to do.

Vocabulary

Un plano de la ciudad
Una lista de hoteles
Tres estrellas
Pension completa
Media pension
El centro comercial
El barrio
Típico

Employee

1 Would he/she like a simple plan of the town which costs nothing, or a map of the region, including town plan, which costs 10 pesetas?

2 Offer a hotel list. What are their requirements (four-star, three-star, two-star, one-star, etc., full/half board, near sea, etc.)?

  Offer to telephone and make booking.

3 What kind of shops (supermarket outside town, new hypermarket with smart shops, old picturesque quarter with small shops, etc.)?

  What kind of restaurant do they want?

4 How old is child?

  Mention beach activities: boat excursions, sailing, tennis.
  In town: museum, gardens, cinema, castle a few kilometres away. Is information required about any of these?

Situation 44

You are on holiday in Spain with your family, including your elderly aunt. You go to a seaside town on the east coast and call at the *Oficina de turismo.* You speak to an employee at the enquiry desk.

1   Ask about the availability of hotel accommodation.

2   Say that a lift is essential because of your aunt.

3   Ask them to telephone to make a booking for you.

4   Ask about restaurants in the locality.

Vocabulary

Reservar
Un ascensor
Una tía
La montaña

Employee

1 Find out how many in party, length of stay, how they are travelling.

Ask what kind of accommodation required: full/half board, bath, shower, etc.

2 Ask what grade of hotel required: only two-star hotels and above have lifts.

Do they want a view of the sea or of the mountains? In town or out of town?

3 You agree to telephone, but explain that some hotels may be full. Would they mind being separated, either on different floors of the same hotel or in different hotels?

4 Either offer a list of restaurants or recommend several different restaurants.

At the airport

Situation 45

It is 2.30 p.m. You have arrived at an airport in the south of Spain and had arranged to meet a friend there arriving from northern Spain. You go to the information desk and speak to the clerk.

1 Ask what time your friend's flight is due to arrive.

2 Ask what time coaches leave the airport to go to the city centre.

3 Ask if there has been a message for you.

4 Thank him/her and ask where coaches leave from.

Vocabulary

El vuelo
Un autocar
El centro de la ciudad
Un recado
La sala

Clerk

1 Say flight should arrive at 2.45 p.m. but it will be one hour late.

2 Coaches to city centre run every half hour.

3 Ask his/her name. Yes, there is a message. When asked, say friend doesn't want him/her to wait, but will get in touch later to arrange new rendezvous.

4 They leave from just outside the main hall. Can he/she see them?

Situation 46

You are at a large Spanish airport, waiting to catch a plane back to London. You hear an announcement, but cannot understand it. You decide to ask another passenger waiting near you if he or she can explain.

1 Say that you could not understand the announcement. It was too fast.

2 Say that you are afraid of missing your plane.

3 Say that someone has told you that it is foggy in London, and that your flight will probably be delayed.

4 Ask if he/she will tell you when the departure time of your flight is announced.

Vocabulary

Un anuncio
Perder
Con retraso
Hay niebla
Despegar

Passenger

1 Say that announcement was for passengers to Germany. Is that where he/she is going?

2 Which flight does he/she want to catch?

3 Say that you have just heard that the fog has cleared. Is the weather often bad in London?

Does he/she live in London? If not, where?

You will be staying in the centre of London. How can you get there from Heathrow airport?

4 Ask about his/her stay in Spain. What did he/she enjoy most?

At the customs

Situation 47

You are going through customs on the way home from a holiday. You speak to a customs officer.

1 Say that you have nothing to declare.

2 Ask why you are having to wait so long, as you have a train to catch.

3 Ask whether he/she wants to look inside your suitcases.

4 Say that the case he/she is looking at is not yours.

Vocabulary

Declarar
La maleta
En el extranjero
Verificar
Una camara fotográfica
Pertenecer

Customs officer

1 Didn't he/she buy anything abroad?

2 There is a lot of luggage to check. How many pieces of luggage has he/she?

3 Ask him/her to open a suitcase. Why are there five cameras in this suitcase?

4 Ask why he/she was carrying it if it was not his/hers.
Ask his/her name and ask him/her to go with you.

Situation 48

During a long holiday in Spain you go to Portugal for a few days, and on returning to Spain, where you will be staying for another month, you go through the Spanish customs, and speak to a customs officer.

1 Declare what you have bought in Portugal.

2 Say where and when you bought your camera before going to Portugal.

3 Ask how much you will have to pay for your extra bottles of wine.

4 Ask if you can pick up your suitcases and leave.

Vocabulary

Portugal
El tabaco
El vino
El perfume
El reloj
Los derechos de aduana
La botella

Customs officer

1   Ask if that is everything, mentioning anything that may have been forgotten – wine, perfume, tobacco, etc.

2   Check that the watch he/she is wearing is not new.

3   Say the duty will be 80 pesetas a bottle. Ask how many bottles.

4   Check on which luggage belongs to him/her before allowing him/her to pass.

At the camp site

Situation 49

You are camping in Spain with your family, and your younger sister falls ill. The doctor arrives, and as you are the only member of the family who speaks Spanish, you speak to the doctor.

1 Say your sister is feeling unwell.

2 Say you think it is something she ate yesterday.

3 Say she slept very badly last night, and she seems feverish.

4 Say your parents are very worried, and ask if you should go back home.

Vocabulary

Sentirse enfermo
Tener fiebre
Tomar la temperatura
Estar preocupado
Volver
El dolor
Grave
Hospedarse en

Doctor

1 Ask what the trouble is. Has she a pain, and if so, where?

2 Ask what she had to eat yesterday, and if she has eaten anything today.

3 Ask if she has had her temperature taken.

Ask how old she is and if she is often ill.

4 Say that it isn't necessary to go home. It's nothing serious, but she needs rest. Could they perhaps stay in a hotel?

Situation 50

You are on holiday in Spain with your family, and you are the only one who speaks Spanish. You have just arrived at a camp site, and you go into the camp office, where you speak to an employee.

1 Say who you are, and that you have booked for a week.

2 Ask where you can put up your tent.

3 Ask if you can buy fresh bread and milk on the site.

4 Ask where the toilets and showers are.

Vocabulary

Armar una tienda
La ducha

Employee

1 Check on how booking was made, and on people in family.

2 Say that it isn't far, and that you will accompany them.

3 Say there is milk in camp shop, and a baker visits site at 8 o'clock every morning. Ask if he/she would prefer to shop at the nearest supermarket. If so, does he/she know where it is?

4 Toilets and showers are 25 metres away, on the right. Is there anything else they want to know?

At the post office

Situation 51

While on holiday in Spain, you go into a post office, and speak to the counter clerk.

1   Ask how much the postage is to England.

2   Ask for four stamps, and ask how long it takes for a letter to get to England.

3   Say that you have a parcel to send to England.

4   Ask if you can borrow a pen to fill in the form, and ask how much it costs.

Vocabulary

Un sello
Un paquete
Llenar
Un formulario
La aduana
Una postal
¿Me presta . . . ?
El contenido
El valor

Counter clerk

1 Ask whether it is for letters or postcards. Tell him/her the
different rates.

2 Say a letter takes only a few days, but a postcard takes about
a week.

3 Ask about the contents and value of the parcel, and ask
him/her to fill in a form for the customs.

4 Say the parcel plus stamps costs 485 pesetas.

Situation 52

You are travelling in Spain, and have arranged for your family to send letters for you to collect at the local post office. You go to the post office, and speak to the counter clerk.

1 Ask whether there is any mail for you.

2 Ask whether there will be another delivery today as you are expecting another letter.

3 Buy stamps for the letters and postcards you have to post.

4 You have a parcel to post.

Vocabulary

Correos
La lista de correos
Un documento (de identidad)
Un reparto
Esperar
Volver

Counter clerk

1 Ask what name. There is one letter. Ask for identification.

2 There will be another delivery later in the day. Ask if he/she can call back.

   Ask how long he/she will be staying.

3 How many letters? How many postcards? Where are they going to?

4 Where is the parcel going to? There is a Customs declaration to fill in if it is going out of the country. What is in the parcel, and what is its value?

At the police station

Situation 53

You are staying with a family in Spain. You have lost your purse, but are not sure where you have lost it. You go to the local police station and speak to a policeman.

1   Ask if he can help you as you have lost your purse.

2   Give a description of the purse and its contents (money and air ticket to London).

3   Say that you have to go back to London in a few days' time and don't know what to do.

4   Ask what you should do about your lost air ticket.

Vocabulary

Perder
Un bolso
Un billete de avion
La oficina de objetos perdidos

Policeman

1   Ask where and when it was lost.

2   Ask what enquiries have been made so far, i.e. shops,
    transport, etc.

3   Suggest he/she goes to the lost property office.

    Ask for details of the Spanish family as they could send the
    purse on to England if it is found.

4   Suggest he/she telephones the airport to explain about the air
    ticket.

    Say that you will do your best to find the purse, but you are not
    very hopeful.

Situation 54

You are staying in a Spanish town when you discover that you have lost your wallet which contained nearly all your money. You go to the police station to report your loss, and speak to a policeman.

1 Tell him about losing your wallet.

2 Say you have lost nearly all your money and that you don't know what to do.

3 Ask him if he has any suggestions to make.

4 Say that you will have to go home sooner than you had intended.

Vocabulary

Una cartera de bolsillo
Aconsejar
Un pasaporte
La Embajada Británica
La chequera
Un cheque de viaje
Una agencia de viajes
El seguro

Policeman

1 Sympathise and find out exactly when and where it was lost, and what he/she has done about it. Establish contents of wallet.

2 Has he/she still got passport and airline tickets? If yes, say there should be no problem. If no, suggest he/she contact British Embassy and airline.

3 Ask if he/she has a credit card or a cheque book, or any traveller's cheques. If yes, suggest going to a bank. If no, suggest phoning family or contacting British Embassy.

4 Ask if insured. If so, suggest going to travel agency to make claim.

Staying with a Spanish family

Situation 55

You are staying with a Spanish family by the name of Soto. You go into the kitchen and speak to el señor or la señora Soto.

1   Ask if you can help with the washing up.

2   Say that you are enjoying your stay very much and hope that he/she isn't too tired with the extra work.

3   Say that you want to go and buy something in town. Is there anything he/she needs from the shops?

4   Ask what time you need to be back for lunch.

Vocabulary

Ayudar
Fregar los platos
Un paño de cocina
En el pueblo

El señor/La señora Soto

1 Thank him/her. Does he/she know where the tea towel is?
What does he/she do to help at home?

2 You're not too tired, and it's a pleasure having him/her.
Would he/she like to come again next year?

3 Does he/she know where the baker's is, as you would like some bread and cakes.

4 Lunch is at 2.30 p.m. Don't be late, as you will be going out in the car later. Would he/she like to come?

Situation 56

You are in Spain, staying with a Spanish family. They have all gone out, leaving you alone, as you wanted to write a letter. The telephone rings and you answer it.

1 Ask who it is.

2 Say where everybody has gone.

3 Ask if you can take a message, or if the caller would prefer to ring back.

4 Say what time the family will probably be back.

Vocabulary

Volvar a telefonear
Un proyecto

Caller

1   Say it is el señor or la señora Garcia, and ask to speak to el señor or la señora Morales.

Ask who is speaking.

2   Ask why he/she has been left alone in the house.

3   Ask if he/she knows what the family has planned for Saturday evening, as you would like to invite them for dinner.

Would he/she like to come too?

4   Ask if he/she is enjoying the stay, and how much longer he/she will be in Spain.

Will he/she ask el señor or la señora Morales to phone when they come back?

Situation 57

You have been staying with a Spanish family, and would like to buy them a present before you go home. You discuss this with a friend.

1 Ask if he/she has any ideas about a suitable present.

2 Say you have 600 pesetas to spend.

3 Find out where the best shops are.

4 Ask if he/she will come and help you choose something.

Vocabulary

Gastar
Delicioso/rico
El juguete
El juego
El almacén

Friend

1 Ask if they all like chocolates. If yes, say you know where to buy delicious chocolates. If no, suggest flowers, or toys for the children. What do they like to play with?

2 Say little cars and some games are not expensive.

3 The best shops are the department stores in the town centre. When will he/she have time to go there?

4 Agree, but you can only manage a lunch hour. Will that be all right? If so, arrange to meet.

At the bank

Situation 58

You are in a bank in Spain, and speak to the bank clerk.

1   Ask if you can change some English money into Spanish pesetas.

2   Ask what the rate of exchange is.

3   Ask if you can use your credit card in Spain.

4   Ask where the cash desk is.

Vocabulary

¿A cómo está el cambio de la libra?
Un documento
La caja
Hacer cola
Pagar al contado

Bank clerk

1 He/she can change money if he/she has proof of identity.

2 Give the current rate. How much does he/she want to change?

3 In many places it is possible: look out for the sign. But it is often cheaper to pay cash.

4 On his/her right, where there is a queue.

Ask how long he/she is staying in Spain, what visits he/she has made, etc.

At home

Situation 59

You are a Spanish boy or girl. You go into the living-room at home, where your father/mother is working, and speak to him/her.

1 Say that you are going to see a friend.

2 Say that if anyone phones you will be at Rosa's house.

3 Ask what time dinner will be ready.

4 Ask what is for dinner.

Vocabulary

Listo
El pollo
Una legumbre

Father/mother

1   Has he/she finished homework?

2   Who is he/she expecting to phone?

Who is Rosa?

3   Dinner will be ready at 8.30 p.m. Can he/she be home by
    8 p.m., as you will need some help?

4   Chicken for dinner, but you haven't yet decided what
    vegetables. What would he/she like?

On holiday in Spain

Situation 60

You are on holiday in Spain, and have run short of money. You decide to ask a Spanish friend for help.

1   Say that you have telephoned your parents to ask them to send you some more money.

2   Ask if you can borrow some money.

3   Say you will pay back the loan when the money arrives from your parents.

4   Apologise for having to ask for money.

Vocabulary

Prestar
Pedir prestado
Reembolsar
Sacar dinero